Kevin McCloud's
COLOUR NOW

An expert guide
to choosing colour
for your home

Quadrille
PUBLISHING

Contents

WHY I WROTE THIS BOOK

With this book my aim was to put together a balanced range of interesting, powerful colours – compiled into a collection of colour palettes – that can provide a useful working tool for the designer, decorator, homeowner and anybody else who is turned on by the emotional power of colour.

In my previous book on colour, *Choosing Colours*, the palettes were largely sourced from the natural world and from historical artefacts and schemes such as Italian medieval painted chests and 1960s Volkswagen camper van paint colours. The palettes in that book were collections of colours that best exemplify their time or place and which are powerful by association.

Here, in this accessible follow up, the emphasis is slightly different. That isn't to say that the associative power of colour is no longer important. Rather, in this book I hope to show you how one relatively small (albeit carefully selected) range of colours can, perhaps unexpectedly, supply you with pretty much all the elements of colour you'll ever need.

A powerful palette to my mind is one that is not just a set of interesting or strong colours: it's something that has its own identity above those colours and which can trigger strong associations, sometimes in our subconscious, of a time or place or emotion. A single colour can of course trigger such associations by itself, like a Miles Davis solo can. The palette, on the other hand, can work like a full orchestra.

The one thing this book definitely does not profess to be is in any way universal. It does not cover every colour model or every example of a 'balanced' colour scheme. Instead it simply aims to demonstrate a range of colours that will provide you with everything you need to make your interior design balanced – colours that will flatter each other and you, and will make your environment a more civilised place. I hope you enjoy looking at them and using them.

HOW THIS BOOK WORKS

In this book, you will find a collection of 120 colours put together in different ways to form 67 groups, or palettes. Together these 120 colours form the colour collection that can be found on pages 154–5. The colours that form this collection – ordered in terms of colour and intensity – have been chosen to complement one another, to be easy on the eye and to form a harmonious, balanced whole. At least, that was the plan.

I could simply have provided you with a list of interesting colours, but that would have been pointless. The choice of any colour must be an informed one. We use colour in an informed way, exploiting its perceived value and associations to convey unspoken and unwritten ideas and emotions. So, all the colours in this book come from somewhere, and each is connected to a thing or place or time. Many have their origins in the landscape, in the earth itself and the natural dyes that produced the first colours for decorative use. They are also all complex pigments that have a long history of being used in decoration. And yet, all these colours, perhaps because of their complexity, perhaps simply because they have such real personality, remain relevant. Within this book you will find tints that have been used in both seventeenth century interiors and on the walls of iconic contemporary art galleries.

As individually interesting as each of these colours may be in isolation, it is when they work together in combination that they are able to convey a powerful message – either very directly, or in a more subtle way. It is for this reason that every colour in this book is shown as part of a group of colours, a palette.

You can extract colours from this book in a variety of ways: by copying an entire palette and employing the full force of any association or subtle value it may have; by drawing on a smaller group of colours; or by using just one colour. It really is up to you.

The palettes themselves have been numbered for practicality's sake, but have consciously not been named according to their sources.

This provides the hidden advantage of removing any prejudice you might have about a colour or arrangement of colours. You could be very drawn to a set of colours for, say, your living room, or a project, or an ad campaign you are running. Were that palette to occur in a section marked 'Wall Colours' and be called 'Early Jericho', you might be put off using it even before you had finished reading the title. Better to thumb through the book and just mark the palettes that catch your eye, than be bogged down and blinkered by words.

HOW TO FIND A PAINT COLOUR

Every one of the colour swatches featured in this book can be matched to a Fired Earth paint colour. On pages 156–158 you will find a list that details which of the colours in the paint collection is used in which palette. You will also find details of how each of these colours can be easily matched to a Fired Earth paint colour. Alternatively you could use the swatches to match to a paint of your choice in a paint shop.

A NOTE ON THE COLOUR REPRODUCTION

National and international standard colours have been matched by the comparison of Hexachrome® colour swatches with approved control references (for example the colour control atlases of the Natural Color System®, or NCS®, and the International Organization for Standardization, or ISO, references) and cross-matched with accompanying published Munsell Books of Colour, Lab or NCS® colour references. See colour model 4 on page 152 for a fuller understanding of the Hexachrome® printing process used to produce this book.

the colour palettes

1

'There are always a myriad of colour choices that will work in any situation, as long as the tonal value is appropriate.'
Gaye Adams

Never underestimate the importance of putting red and green together. They are complementaries and so fire off each other, even when a little muted as they are here. For centuries they've battled in a love-hate relationship, ever since they were formally introduced to each other in the designs of seventeenth-century Murghal textiles. I'm not making this up. These beautiful fabrics, destined to influence designs into the twenty first century, were decorated with rose and leaf patterns on an off-white ground. Exactly the colours, in fact, shown on this page. This is the power of history.

the palettes **13**

1

3

4

14 the palettes

2

'Colour is sensibility in material form, matter in its primordial state.'
Yves Klein

Here's another game played between red and green, and another good example of Gaye Adams' observation (see page 12) that you can put any number of colours together, even complementaries, providing that they are tonally similar: that is, they are equally intense, or greyed, or tinted or dirtied. What's important is that they hang out together with the same attitude.

And I'm a fan of the dado. I mean, using a band of colour on the lower part of the wall, a practice that's been around since at least 6,000 years ago in Jericho. It is a practical solution for hiding the dirt and a way of introducing strong colour to a room without overpowering it or you.

5

6

3

'Why do two colours, put one next to the other, sing? Can one really explain this? No. Just as one can never learn how to paint.'
Pablo Picasso

This palette is another good example of tonally matched colours. The complementary touch comes in the orange-brown. Cover this swatch up with a piece of white paper and the palette becomes altogether more serious and formal. Cover up the blue swatch and the palette loses its eccentricity.

As the picture shows, you don't always need paint or fabric to provide the complementary colour effect. A vase will do. In this case, a bowl of oranges would have had the same effect. Add one lime and a sprig of mint and you've got the gist of the whole palette.

5   6

4

'On the whole, the modern palette is the same as the one used by the artists of Pompeii. I mean it has not been enriched. The ancients used earths, ochres, and ivory-black – you can do anything with that palette.'
Pierre-Auguste Renoir

Brown is a sneaky colour. It can materialize out of grey, red, green, purple or orange. Two complementary paint colours, like red and green for example, or blue and orange, will usually make a kind of gooey brown, and the examples of artists using this formula, or overpainting, say, green foliage on a red ground, are legion.

But for intensity and character it is best to rely on traditional clay pigments like burnt sienna, raw and burnt umber, Pozzuoli red or Vandyke brown (made in fact from pitch). These pigments convey brown across the gamut of its schizophrenic characters.

Here a cool, purplish brown is used as the referee between a related earthy red and the more delicate Chinese greens. You could say – as I like to – that it anchors the colour scheme.

5

'He had that curious love of green, which in individuals
is always the sign of a subtle artistic temperament, and
in nations is said to denote a laxity, if not a decadence
of morals.'
Oscar Wilde

Of course, you don't need to use complementary colours to funk up
a scheme. The blues and greens on this page are all from the same
neighbourhood on the colour wheel: bluish greens and greenish
blues. What's neat here is the way in which the scheme has been
entirely devised in paint and the leather colour has been
reproduced here and there on the walls. Can't find the fabric or
wallpaper to match that 1940s armchair? Easy. Just paint your
own. And don't bother about making it neat.

6

'Colours are promiscuous. They get infected by their neighbours.'
Paul Richard

Now it might seem obvious to you, but it is worth illustrating just how a dash of colour can wake up a moribund idea. Cover up the greenish chairs in the picture and the room looks dead. Reveal them and it looks a mite healthier.

What's not so obvious is that using one strong colour in a monochrome scheme is difficult to do. This green is yellowish and mixed with a little grey to bring it closer to the deathly pallor of the room. A red or blue or orange would need to be equally toned in order to strike up a friendship here.

7

'If time were a colour, I bet it would be a tasteful off-white.'
Greg Parrish

Now this is more like it. Here, the greens are used to balance a whole range of cleverly put together shades of grey – some warm and brownish, some cooler. The green injects some life into this scheme; yellow would do a similar thing, but a tiny dose of blue or red here would just look bland.

8

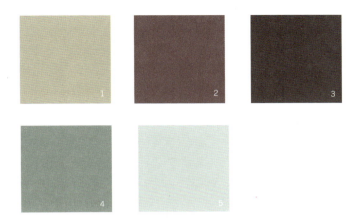

'I'm intrigued that one can recognize different parts of the world solely by the particular colour of the water.'
Leonard Mizerek

So what colour is water? When it is frozen and you're looking deep into a glacier, it takes on a luminous turquoise colour which, sadly, when used in paint suggests only municipal swimming pools. In the River Nile, it is the colour of the River Nile; a famous green, eau-de-nil, which is the colour of the palest green swatch here (5).

The seas of the world, by contrast, are every different blue imaginable. And the colour of a still pond is the colour chosen for this bathroom. And yet here it looks just fine because it has been contained and used on only one simple architectural element. That's a good lesson.

9

'If the tones are balanced, you can use almost any colour.'
Janine Parsons

Up until now we've seen green work with its complementary, red, in a number of ways. We've seen it controlled by brown – a strong anchoring colour – and we've seen it used as a form of decorative adrenaline to wake up dull, neutral and monochrome palettes. Now, for the first time, purple gets a look-in.

It may take some time to digest this fact, but purple in one form or another (you can call it mauve, or violet or even puce, I don't care) is as strong an anchoring colour as brown. It can hold a palette together. And for the purposes of decorating a room, at least, it can be your salvation.

10

'At one side of the palette there is white, at the other black; and neither is ever used neat.'
Winston Churchill

This palette goes to show that you can get away with several greys and off-whites together all from the same area of the palette. These tints are all slightly muddied and green-tinged. Not an appealing description, admittedly, but a brilliant combination in use. Warmer greys tend to need a little spiking up, with some brown, purple or complementary colours. Not these.

11

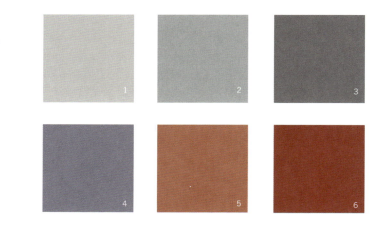

'Colour is crucial in painting, but it is very hard to talk about. There is almost nothing you can say that holds up as a generalization, because it depends on too many factors: size, modulation, the rest of the field, a certain consistency that colour has with forms, and the statement you're trying to make.'

Roy Lichtenstein

Having said that, look at what happens if you introduce some sunny warm colours to some austere cool greenish greys. The colours of amber and honey. The whole thing lifts off. This is a very smart and complex palette: it doesn't use much white, nor any strong complementary, but is all the stronger for it.

12

'I see a green tree. And to me it is green. And you would call the tree green also. And we would agree on this. But is the colour you see as green the same colour I see as green?'
Carson McCullers

One of the great modern architectural obsessions is that of 'bringing the outside in'. At least that's what clients like to call it. Architects call it the 'dissolving of boundaries'. Whatever. To achieve the effect, you could build your walls out of glass or fresh air. Or you could just paint an inside wall green.

In the 1980s, the respected anthropologist Desmond Morris conducted some interesting research that revealed the most popular colour choice for hallways was green. Not so much a hallway as a hillway then. Should you want to do the same, this little palette provides the perfect template.

5

13

'It is not the form that dictates the colour, but the colour that brings out the form.'
Hans Hofmann

On page 149 you'll find a colour model that corresponds reasonably precisely with how we see the world. There, blue-green has a place and its complementary colour is orange proper. Now, I might be stretching things here but the colours of light timbers tend to be muddied beigish tones of orange and orange-yellow, which makes them pretty good complementary colours for the shade of greenish blue used on the chair. Want pine to look good? Then put it, as here, with teal.

14

'Almost without exception, blue refers to the domain of abstraction and immateriality.'
Wassily Kandinsky

There is a wonderful relationship between brown and blue. Frankly, it is better than the one between brown and green – colours that argue for the same territory on the planet. But sky and earth just seem to get on. This is a relationship that can be explored with many different browns and blues, and is something that I've been able to do in this book.

Brown is an anchoring colour, for obvious associative reasons, and is therefore, I suppose, appropriate for a bedroom, a nest. The use of it with blue in the adjacent bathroom is just about the most appropriate colour combination for an en-suite.

15

'There is not one blade of grass, there is no colour in this world that is not intended to make us rejoice.'
John Calvin

Often the most stimulating colour combinations come from strong cultural influences, from the built environment, food, or from nature. Here we have a pretty worldly palette, one of stone and sea and earth and sky.

1   2   3   4

16

'Everything that you can see in the world around you presents itself to your eyes only as an arrangement of patches of different colours.'
John Ruskin

Just as there are a million sources of inspiration in the living natural world, so too the dead natural world has its moments. Like the post-conflagration colours of charred and smouldering remains, for example.

Perhaps unwittingly, the owners of this room seem to have based their colour scheme on what met them every morning in the grate of their woodburner: the colours of ash, clinker and half-burnt wood. It is a clever palette.

17

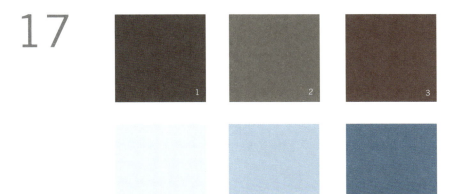

'Seek the strongest colour effect possible; the content is of no importance.'
Henri Matisse

'Oh yes it is.'
Kevin McCloud

Now and again, a colour palette pops up which teasingly, almost wilfully, seems to push a colour relationship to the limits, to the extremes of tolerance. And I think this is one. Superficially it can be seen as being in 'good taste': it explores the blue and brown relationship and keeps insisting and repeating on those colours – in the floor tiles, through the broken colour on the walls that seems to be hanging on by willpower alone, through the absurd painted feet and the dirt-coloured bath. This is the kind of combination that has been worked through with an almost vindictive meticulousness. The blue is a good French blue, the brown is a cool raw umber. They make a good pair, if you can tolerate such a powerful duo.

18

'True perfection seems imperfect, yet it is perfectly itself.'
Lao Tzu in the *Tao Te Ching*

In the previous palette, the broken colour on the walls made an important contribution to the overall colour scheme. It pushed the colour, seemingly, into the wall and brought it some life. Often though, broken colour effects can be overdone. Thankfully, the fashion for them that ran through the 1980s and 1990s has died a death, leaving us with merely the epitaphs of the odd colourwashed hairdressers or rag-rolled Victorian themed pub toilet.

That's not to say, however, that broken or 'distressed' colour should never be used. Oh no. In this room, every painted surface is imperfect, knackered or rubbed through. It might be those pieces of bonsai broccoli but I could swear that there is a Tao serenity in the collection of all these broken blues and woody browns – not just a representation of earth and sky, but more a meditation on the crumbling quality of earth and the ethereal mist of sky.

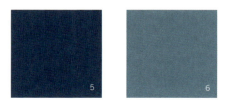

19

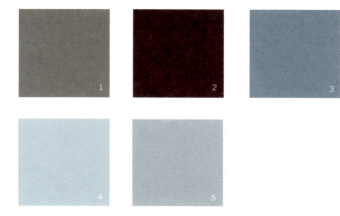

'The sun is so terrific here that it seems to me as if the objects were silhouetted not only in black and white, but in blue, red, brown and violet.'
Paul Cezanne (to Camille Pissarro)

This is the first meeting in this book of two strong ideas, the joining of two anchors, brown and purple. Admittedly the brown arrives in the form of a chunk of driftwood masquerading as a table, as well as in the salty-looking floor. And the purple isn't much to look at either; it is more of a dusty grey, really. But together these colours control the odd liquorice assortment of blues, black and white. They would sort out any colour combination, frankly. Brown and purple together are a formidable team, able to bring any restless and aggressive bunch of yobbish colours into line.

20

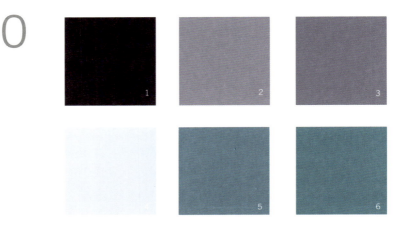

'Colours are light's suffering and joy.'
Johann Wolfgang von Goethe

From the work I've done in schools, I've been able to form a few important conclusions about colour preferences. One of these is that, yes, girls like pink. But, this is only the case until about the age of seven or eight, when purple in one form or another takes premier place. Hence the wide range of girls' toys available in an ambiguous lilac-pink colour. There will always be, in addition, a renegade, gothic element who – from as early an age as six – prefer black.

All of which may explain the appeal of this palette, a delicate mix of greenish blues, pinks, purple, lilac and black. This scheme has a highly inclusive feminine appeal. Of course I wouldn't be seen dead anywhere near it, but then I'm a man and like the colour of engine oil, diggers and concrete.

21

'Oh! "darkly, deeply, beautifully blue",
as someone somewhere sings about the sky.'
Lord Byron

Until the mid-twentieth century, synthetic colour was predominantly dependent on rocks and plants. The coal-tar chemistry of the 1860s and 1870s had unlocked new dye colours like Mauve, Methyl Violet, Magenta and Fuchsin, but frankly if you wanted a paint it was made out of ground-up minerals – usually compounds of metal like cobalt, copper, iron and chrome.

And if you wanted to dye cloth, you were reliant on plant extracts like madder for red, or woad or indigo for blue. Woad and indigo are chemically identical dyes and are produced from related plants. The dyes for the bedspread and the paint for the walls are still being produced using traditional indigo and woad by small craft workshops, though synthetic indigo is now widely available.

But the association of these blues with plant power persists. Perhaps, then, there's no better colour to put them with than that of unbleached linen.

22

'We get used to a certain kind of colour of form or format, and it's acceptable. And to puncture that is sticking your neck out a bit. And then pretty soon, that's very acceptable.'
Lee Krasner

There is no such thing as true black. Well, perhaps there is the sensation of looking into an Anish Kapoor vessel lined with black velvet. Or staring at a black cat in a coal bunker; that must be close. Everything else, however, is leached with a drop of colour. A filament light bulb will make a black paint appear brown, a Northern blue sky will turn it inky blue. A painted room will reflect its colour onto black and change it.

So give up on searching for true black and use a very dark colour instead – it will be much more yielding and tolerant of all kinds of nonsense. The colours in this room are riotous but they are told to shut up and behave by the powerful funeral parlour blue.

23

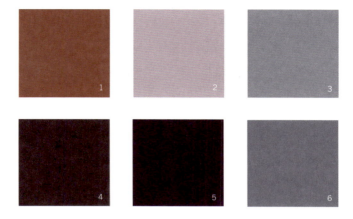

'*Colour is the language of the poets. It is astonishingly lovely. To speak it is a privilege.*'
Keith Crown

Looking at palette numbers 7 and 10 (see pages 24 and 31 respectively), you can see how well greenish greys work in buildings. They have some life and complexity about them that bluish greys lack. Bluish greys are military and came into their own as World War I battleship camouflage. However the really interesting greys – the ones used here – are those made with purple. They have a warm, brownish cast that flatters flesh tones and brings natural woody materials to life. They are not popular. But they should be.

24

'With the brush we merely tint, while the imagination alone produces colour.'
Theodore Gericault

A few of the quotations from artists that are used in this book talk about tonal value. That is, getting a group of colours to work by making them equally grey, or dirty, or dusty looking. With paint this usually means adding another colour like raw umber plus white, or a drop of red or black. One of the easiest ways to achieve this tonal balance is to tint a whole batch of different colours with white to make a packet of pastels. Got some old tins of paint you don't know what to do with? Add some white and you'll have a palette of colours that look as though they were designed to go together.

25

'Thought, as we have so far described it, is what it is by virtue of becoming all things, while there is another which is what it is by virtue of making all things: this is a sort of positive state like light; for in a sense light makes potential colours into actual colours.'
Aristotle

By far the hardest colours to get right are the tints of the four optical primaries (red, blue, yellow and green) from the colour model on page 149. As most modern paints are coloured with a limited range of powerful synthetic dyes, getting a pale green, pale blue, cream or pink that doesn't look as though it was made in a children's toy factory can seem to be an impossibility.

But the interesting colours are those made with muddy, traditional earth pigments or complex arrangements of colourants. The best pinks – those that change colour under different lighting conditions – are those on the cusp of red and purple, made with red oxide pigments. The best yellows or creams – those that will withstand bluish Northern light and never look green – are those made with, or those that approximate, yellow ochre. Now you know.

26

'My favorite colour is a soft shade of "Outright Totality," but often I am lured by hues of "Habitat" or a stunning tone of "Subconscious".'
Jacques Vesery

Black and white, when set down in a room, can seem the most brutal and unfriendly combination. Fine in a Malevich painting but cold as an environment. Better to mix a near-black with an off-white. Or with beige. Or black and pink. Or pink and greenish grey – an outstanding way of combining complementaries by tinting one (red) and toning the other (green).

Or why not, as here, just do all of the above?

27

'I would start with a colour, a form, and it begins dictating to me what's needed in terms of colour as well as form.'
Lee Krasner

Sometimes colours become so washed out and delicate that it becomes hard to recognize and reproduce them. Finish plaster or 'Sirapite' to give it one trade name, is brown when wet, but dries back to a pale, earthy pink. Needless to say it works nicely with the uniform colour of the concrete (bath) and the wood (ladder), but also anything else with a single, uniform colour for that matter (such as the jug, soap, and rubber plug).

Really, though, what we're looking at here is an extension of an idea on page 62, that of the green/pink complementary battle which rages through colour. Here, it is expressed just as an echo, in the colours of pink clay and greenish cement.

28

'*The colour of the object illuminated partakes of the colour of that which illuminates it.*'
Leonardo da Vinci

If you live in the Northern Hemisphere, then you'll be used to blue light – the light that clouds let through. Britain has, apparently, more low cloud than any other European country. British artists and decorators have consequently become expert at handling colours that vibrate in that blue spectrum light. Cusp colours like bluey/greeny/browny/gooey or cool pink. Or blue, obviously. Or almost any earth pigment for that matter.

After all, colours do not exist as properties of objects or surfaces. They are figments of our imagination, a response to light reflected off a surface; the light that isn't absorbed by that surface. Change the light and the colour changes too.

29

'Colour in certain places has the great value of making the outlines and structural planes seem more energetic.'
Antonio Gaudi

A complementary relationship can define a space. Here we have two triangles of colour, both muted versions of the complementaries purple and green-yellow, whose relationship does just that.

30

'It is not by his mixing and choosing, but by the shapes of his colours, and the combination of those shapes, that we recognize the colourist. Colour becomes significant only when it becomes form.'
Clive Bell

The purple-green tussle seems to be even stronger in this image than on the previous page. But as the yellow-green is weaker and more dissipated with grey, so the purple grows stronger. And it has brought its neighbours along too: blue and pink, both of which, appear slightly neutered here. The blue is greyed and the pink is broken up with pattern. The grey-green, meanwhile, has some back up in the colours of the mirror surrounds and linen.

Bet you never thought it was such carnage out there.

31

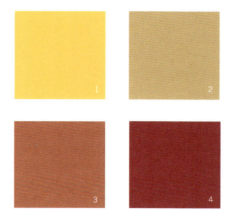

'The West is colour. Its colours are animal rather than vegetable, the colours of earth and sunlight and ripeness.'
Jessamyn West

White and black may not form a particularly inspired combination, but white plus colour does – a bit like applying blobs of hue to a primed canvas. But if even this is too much trouble, why not make life even easier and safer for yourself and only paint the recesses? This scheme is about as safe as you can get because the colour isn't really allowed out of the box. And it is not as though these are brilliant chromatic hues; they are earthy, complex versions of red and yellow. Personally, I'd be tempted to splurge at least one of them across a wall.

32

'The picture will have charm when each colour is very unlike the one next to it.'
Leon Battista Alberti

You can bring every colour to one tonal level by adding white or black or grey or brown. Or you can add some of that colour's complementary. And that's what's happened here. It is as though each colour has been given a dusting of sherbet to lighten and sweeten it. Thinking about it, and to use another confectionery analogy, these all have the colours of boiled sweets with the sugar sucked off, from pear drops to cough sweets.

But there's more, because just as these colours have been seemingly dropped into place in the upholstery, so the walls have also been daubed with blocks of similar colours. The result is almost abstract, a field of coloured shapes.

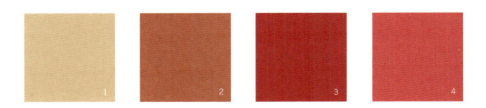

5 6 7 8

33

'He who knows how to appreciate colour relationships, the influence of one colour on another, their contrasts and dissonances, is promised an infinitely diverse imagery.'
Sonia Delaunay

Speaking as I was on the previous page about tonality, I might add that 'tonality' is more important than colours 'matching'. The carpet here, out of nine colours, shares only four with the needlework, which in turn shares none with the sofa or the lamp base, which shares one with the carpet. The wall isn't speaking to any of them and yet – through the magic of complementary colour optics – it throws all the others forward. Tonally, these colours all sit about the same distance back from their respective hues. Not in the cheap seats, more front row of the Upper Circle.

I also have to emphasize how important scatter cushions are in colour schemes. Buy them before you do anything else and then design a colour scheme around them. Paint will give you most colour choice, upholstery the least. Cushions can synthesize an entire scheme brilliantly. As can crochet, for that matter.

3 4 5 6

34

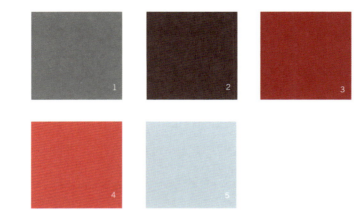

'Blue is the only colour which maintains its own character in all its tones. It will always stay blue; whereas yellow is blackened in its shades, and fades away when lightened; red when darkened becomes brown, and diluted with white is no longer red, but another colour – pink.'
Raoul Dufy

This stripey scheme plays around with earth reds, fixes them with a brownish grey and a dark brown and then adds the magic ingredient – a cool, powder blue. That's a surprise.

While the browns anchor the palette and give it some fibre, nothing comes close to the watery, glass-like blue. Used in this combination it is triumphant.

35

'Everything utilitarian needs a little red edge.'
Reno Dakota

There is a fashion for retro schemes and decoration right now that goes under the moniker 'vintage'. Not vintage cars or aircraft (where the term refers to strict chronological criteria) but second-hand clothes that your auntie would put out with the rubbish, 1950s rusting painted chairs, decaying PVC and melamine table tops. The latter are still very serviceable since original 1950s melamine was built to withstand a full outbreak of the Cold War.

The colours that accompany the revival are cool mid-blues, acid yellows, black, washed out browns and strong, dark reds. You'll find more examples of these colours over the next few palettes and their popularity stems not least from the graphics of the 1950s and early 1960s – where crude offset lithography gave images a slightly grey and grubby look.

36

'A certain blue enters your soul. A certain red has an effect on your blood-pressure.'
Henri Matisse

The same powerful red as on page 79, the same washed out blues and light yellows are to be found, alongside other pastels, in the palettes of the 1920s. These colours were also widely adopted in early Modernist buildings. The 1927 Wiessenhofsiedlung housing project in Stuttgart had homes built by Mart Stam, Le Corbusier and Mies van der Rohe and included houses in pale green, cream and lilac. Contemporary photographs only show them in minimalist black and white of course, but colour images of Le Corbusier's white Villa Savoye near Paris (1929) show a lavishly coloured interior.

37

'Of all the hues, reds have the most potency. If there is one electric blue, a dozen reds are so charged. Use them to punctuate white, burn into bronzes, or dynamite black.'
Jack Lenor Larsen

Slabs of colour can give a bland box of a room some real architectural tension. Colour moves in the imagination. Mid- and pale blues appear to recede, reds and oranges advance. Striped patterns cause confusion and optical effects.

This is a clever application of pattern, an enveloping dado of colour to the left and a monolithic slab of grey-green to the right. And of course there's the obligatory (and if you've been reading this book from the beginning, familiar) red-green story going on underneath.

5 6

38

'The coloured planes, as much by position and dimension as by the greater value given to colour, plastically express only relationships and not forms.'
Piet Mondrian

There's nothing like a little de Stijl colouring to brighten up the International Style home, especially when you can do it in mosaic. Painted black lines can appear a little awkward – unless you live in a Huf Haus in which case the black stained timber frame does half the job for you and you can feel as though you're inhabiting a Mondrian painting.

Looking at this image you can begin to see where most of the architectural colouring of the 1980s came from – all white, black and primaries.

5

1   2   3   4

39

'The "pure" red of which certain abstractionists speak does not exist. Any red is rooted in blood, glass, wine, hunters' caps and a thousand other concrete phenomena. Otherwise we would have no feeling toward red and its relations.'
Robert Motherwell

Using lots of related colours in a grid is a simple way of making a scheme interesting and a neat way of not making up your mind. In palette number 5 (see page 20), it was green. Here it is that interesting border that exists between red and pink, of Fuchsin and Magenta and deep red ochre.

To anyone familiar with looking at images on a screen or working with digital photographs, the correlation is obvious. It is like a vast image, blown up and pixellated beyond recognition.

40

'Colour is my day-long obsession, joy and torment.'
Claude Monet

On the list marked 'fastidious obsessions', getting the right fine old French grey comes pretty high up. Technically speaking, if you took some chalk-white casein distemper, added some raw umber and a little raw sienna then you'd be there. Note I didn't mention black, because when you mix black and white the resulting colour is so cold you might as well call it blue. No, for a good grey, go greenish (look at the early palettes in this book) and stick with earth colours.

Alternatively, you could just buy any one of the paint colours above; excellent complex colours that are the tinctorial equivalent of a fine old French wine.

1   2   3   4

41

'I never met a colour I didn't like.'
Dale Chihuly

Red, blue and yellow never looked so good as they did in the late 1950s and early 1960s. Or at least these colours never looked as good as they did in print. From Weetabix packets to Lego colours, from Bird's Custard tins to the interiors of Case Study Houses, the yellows always seemed rich and warm, cloying even. The reds were comforting and solid, the blues at times dark and reassuring, at others light and cerulean.

I don't know if colours can be optimistic, but these primaries tried their best. They gave way to the technical, optical secondary colours of cyan, bright yellow and magenta; though these, unlike the colours here, are not really the sort you'd ask round for a cocktail party.

42

'In Autumn you can take one maple leaf and see almost all the colours of the rainbow in it – although you would need your imagination to see blue.'
Dorthe Eisenhardt

I've written already about the essential usefulness of crochet in colour schemes and how the judicious use of scatter cushions, for example, can make a real difference to the feeling of your home or workplace. It won't surprise you, therefore, to learn that rugs can often do the same thing. The key tactic, as ever, is to choose your rug first, before then matching your paint colours to it. Your friends will think that you put a scheme together and that only then, after extensive research, were you able to 'tie it all together' with your exclusive find. I know that expecting everyone to think in this about-face way stretches credulity, but believe me, it really is how people think.

43

'We never really perceive what colour is physically.'
Josef Albers

The decades of the twentieth century can each be marked by a palette or by a group of palettes. Just as it is possible to talk about 1970s design and 1920s architecture, it is as though each ten-year period decided upon the colours that it wanted to wear. This is of course a completely fanciful idea, but there is nevertheless a sort of colour narrative that runs through the last century.

The grey- and brown-tinged 1930s and 1940s gave way to a tentative exuberance after the war that didn't fully flower until the psychedelia of the mid-1960s. This scheme has its origins somewhere in the 1950s. The yellows, which were often acid, are cool and pale here. So are the blues, for that matter.

44

'*A colour is as strong as the impression it creates.*'
Ivan Albright

It may seem obvious, but it is only when you compare this room with that on the previous page that you realize colour does not have to be defined by association. A colour is just a colour – it doesn't carry any cultural baggage. You can use a National Trust Georgian Organic Split Pea Green in your eighteenth-century parlour or your 1950s semi downstairs toilet. I don't care and neither does any historical paint consultant I know.

Anyway, back to the photo. These are 1950s colours which carry, as a collective palette, all the subtle messages from that period of austerity and restraint. But they are not in a 1950s room. Brilliant. Obvious, you say. But is it only now that I've mentioned it?

45

'Colour is uncontainable. It effortlessly reveals the limits of language and evades our best attempts to impose a rational order on it.'
David Batchelor

Some cultures just get colour; Mediterranean cultures, the cultures of India, China, central and Southern America, of Scandinavia, Siberia, Africa and Micronesia.

Everywhere, in fact, except the Anglo-Saxon cultures of Northern Europe. Perhaps this has something to do with our suspicion of colour's unruliness, its resistance to categorization and nomenclature. Its emotionality.

Other less uptight cultures accept that same disorder – controlling and modulating colour in architecture by placing it in certain places and in certain combinations. By painting the door reveal red, for example.

5   6

46

'A colour called "Pants left in wash"'
Eddie Izzard

There is a vast ocean of rubbish that is talked about historical colours and, as a consequence, many factoids that need to be dispelled. Such as the myth that grubby, muddy paints are historic. They are not. Rather, they just suggest an unfortunate lack of basic domestic hygiene.

Of course, if you want to suggest that yours is an historic home open to the public or you simply happen to enjoy the theatricality of dirtiness, then go ahead and use them. What is true is that traditional pigments – from which all paints used to be made – are complex, interesting and tend not to look flat or plasticky. Oh, and as for names, my favourite eighteenth-century colour has to be one that was known then as 'Gallstone'.

47

'I am attracted to generic or "industrial" colours; paper bag brown, file cabinet gray, industrial green, that kind of thing.'
Robert Mangold

Here's a method for getting a bunch of colours to work well together that could have come straight from a 1948 guide to good housekeeping.

First, select the choicest spring greens, yellows and blues. Add some grey to all of them. Just a half cupful. Add seasoning, simmer and then serve with a thickened brown gravy and a good helping of utility furniture. Animal skins optional.

That should give you a hearty post-war colour scheme. A palette with a nostalgic palate. Remember, add grey and serve with brown. Or add brown and serve with grey. Just as authentic.

48

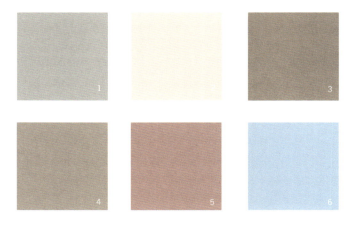

'The whole world, as we experience it visually, comes to us through the mystic realm of colour.'
Hans Hofmann

This book is a supplementary (and frankly a more lighthearted, digestible) follow-up to another volume, *Choosing Colours*, in which the palettes were all taken from historical artefacts and schemes; things like Italian medieval painted chests and 1960s Volkswagen camper van paint colours. The idea was – and is, because you won't shake me from this – that although colours themselves carry very little cultural associations (there have been up to 35 different Ferrari reds for example) when assembled into palettes they can jog the associative memory and carry all kinds of powerful ideas.

One palette that I particularly liked was based on Roman mosaic pavements, taken mainly from examples in the British Museum. If I had seen this photograph first then the whole job would have been much easier, wouldn't it?

49

'Colour is the place where our brain and the universe meet.'
Paul Klee

I know this is a cosy and relaxed room but the colours are those of the building site; of concrete, hard hats and, most interestingly, rust. Rust, iron in its natural, oxidized form, is a host to some of the most bewitching colours on the planet. According to the amount of heat, oxygen and moisture present it can produce a bright yellow ochre or Pozzuoli Red, a cool Red Oxide or a warm Red Ochre, Raw Siena, Burnt siena or greenish Raw Umber (with a little help from some manganese). Even a deep and satisfying synthesized Mars Purple.

Rust is responsible for colouring our sands, clays, rocks and marble. It is the most important colourant in the world.

50

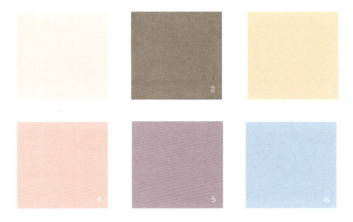

'The mind is excited by what painters refer to as "broken colour", the juxtaposition of two or more colours in a single passage.'
Eric Wiegardt

It is difficult to ascribe a colour to naturally finished wood. A stained finish is easier to match, but then again a woodstain kills the wide variety of colours found in polished timber. Or most natural materials for that matter. But it is possible to 'pull' a collection of colours out of a piece of wood.

Not surprisingly one of those colours will be brown. It is a good colour for anchoring a palette. As is purple. Without either of them this group of swatches would look horribly bland.

51

'*White does not exist in nature.*'
Pierre-Auguste Renoir

Monochrome schemes needn't be made of black and white. In fact, perhaps they shouldn't be, as there's no such thing as true black or true white around us – both will respond to different lighting conditions and become other colours: pale cream, pale blue, dark purple, brown. Both are also subject to the tricks and effects that the retina and the brain play on us. In fact, it's better not to fight what nature does and instead work out a monochrome palette of your own, using greenish greys, brownish greys and earth colours like raw umber and raw sienna (Numbers 6 and 7 here).

Chuck in a few logs and the odd basket for a bit of the 'natural' and your colour scheme is complete.

52

'It seems obvious that colours vary according to lights, because when any colour is placed in the shade, it appears to be different from the same colour which is located in light. Shade makes colour dark, whereas light makes colour bright where it strikes.'
Leon Battista Alberti

This is another example of the way in which, when colours are toned (greyed), tinted (lightened) or shaded (darkened) all to the same degree they sit happily together. It is a bit like organizing a successful party. The best ones are where, by 9pm, everyone has chilled to the same groove.

These colours have chilled. It is as though each one has formed a sugar-frosted coating, a light mist of hoary whiteness. It is a colour effect that was first properly realized by the Della Robbia ceramics family in Renaissance Florence and it works.

53

'If one says "Red"– the name of a colour – and there are fifty people listening, it can be expected that there will be fifty reds in their minds. And one can be sure that all these reds will be very different.'
Josef Albers

Where in a painting it might be possible to see a colour in the abstract, without connotation, to see it naked without the cluttery, cultural baggage it normally carries – that's not usually the case. Even in abstract art, colour comes charged with emotions and associations. When colours sing together they start to tell quite complicated stories. I could recount how this palette reminds me of a girlfriend I had in Stockholm who had red hair and wore green tights most days. Or was it the other way around? Anyway, I just did. You see how powerful the connotations of colour are? Just wait until you start applying colours to objects and surfaces. You become a symphonic composer just like that.

54

'Colour is born of the interpenetration of light and dark.'
Sam Francis

Two palettes ago, the colours got all frosted and pale as they chilled out. Here, a very similar starting grid of colours has picked up some dark grey along the way. The result is that the colours are toned down to a more 'hushed' level. Not so much a party as an afternoon at the library.

It is an idea I often quote but it is quite miraculous how a little grey or black or brown or white, when mixed in, can bring colours together and make them altogether more sociable.

55

'*Mere colour, unspoiled by meaning, and unallied with definite form, can speak to the soul in a thousand different ways.*'
Oscar Wilde

OK. So I admit to having manipulated this palette a little in my favour because I wanted to put this red, this orangy brown and this blue together. They are important medieval pigment colours: those of Saturn red, deep yellow ochre and everyday impure azurite, but not overtly expensive ones. A good red, yellow and blue to help get the jobbing artist by.

But, aha, they are also among the colours used by Volkswagen to paint their camper vans and microbuses of the 1960s onwards. These are the colours, toned with a little brown, which form part of a staple mid-twentieth century range of industrial pigments. They are all just a little off, but far enough to make them very interesting.

56

'The theory of not mixing black to darken colours really needs to be tossed out the window. Used sparingly, black can create wonderful, muted colours.'
Steve Childs

You'd be forgiven for thinking that the rest of the palettes in this book are steering us into the abyss because there's a lot of gloom ahead. I make no apologies for this. From here on, most of the schemes are dark and, in places, muddied. Brown and black aren't so much used as individual anchoring colours in a room but instead are mixed into a number of the other colours. Where brown has been used to mix or as a separate colour it usually occurs with blue – blue and brown being a favourite colour cocktail of mine. But I'm not picky. All kinds of brown work with all kinds of blue. Try it out.

57

'Sometimes when I'm having a colour moment I think to myself, okay what would be the most disgusting colour to add here? Sometimes that "disgusting" can turn out to be "surprising" and "completely gorgeous".'
Angela A'Court

This looks a little like a 1950s interior. You might expect to see Jacques Tati sat in his hat on the sofa. The colours are equally of the same decade. Post-war, serious and seemingly the result of a world pigment shortage that left every can of paint sold after 1946 containing at least 80% left over camouflage paint. Well, that's how it appears to me. Colour (like everything else) had been commandeered and put to military use in the war.

The exceptions are the baby colours, blue and pink. Signals to Britain's newlyweds to get busy. Which they did.

58

'*There are painters who transform the sun into a yellow spot, but there are others who, thanks to their art and intelligence, transform a yellow spot into the sun.*'
Pablo Picasso

Now here's a thing. A fine, soft leather brown, a soft French blue. What a combination. But maybe that's a relationship that needed making less comfortable and a bit zingier with a mustard. Mustard is as mustard does. It adds some vim, eye-wateringly so sometimes.

In fact, the brown-blue relationship in this room is so quiet that you wouldn't give it a moment's notice, would you? The white helps to lift the room of course. But it is the yellow that's doing all the hard work.

59

'*A thimbleful of red is redder than a bucketful.*'
Henri Matisse

Another muted room I hear you say. But no, no! By now, if you study the picture, you'll realize there's a subtle, but quite complex relationship going on here between green and red: in the murky green walls and pink table top; in the cushions (you will know by now the importance of cushions in determining the success of a colour scheme); and in the pouffe.

The transforming object is the pouffe. It is bright and very red, the result being that the colour appears to advance towards you and therefore controls the room. Greens and blues, meanwhile, recede. It is a trick that has been used by National Geographic art editors since National Geographic began, to make pictures look 3-D.

60

'Colour provokes a psychic vibration. Colour hides a power still unknown but real, which acts on every part of the human body.'
Wassily Kandinsky

Just because you want to use pastel colours, don't be fooled into thinking that they need to be clear and obvious. If you add a lot of white to a synthetic red pigment you're going to get a synthetic looking pink. Acid, flat yellow paints will produce acid, flat creams when tinted.

If there is one lesson to be learned from this book, it is not the never-endingness of the red-green dialogue, nor the importance of brown or purple, nor that there is no such thing as white, nor even that difficult colours need to be toned or tinted equally to work together happily. It is that the more complex a colour is, the more it relies on traditional pigments and not synthetic plastics, the more pleasing it will be and the longer that pleasure will last. And what is the point of colour if not to provide pleasure?

61

'Chromophobia is perhaps only chromophilia without the colour.'
David Batchelor

In case you've just picked this book up and happen to have opened it on this page, let me ask you to please turn back one palette and read the text, which is quite important I think. To nail the point of the last sentence home, one of the *bêtes noires* of this volume is the monochrome. Because it is impossible to achieve, given the vagaries of light and materials and the fact that when anybody walks into a monochrome room they wreck the colour scheme.

As a result, anyone who sets out to make a building or a room monochrome is on a hiding to nothing. The grey swatches on this page are not colourless. They each subtly move in the direction of a colour. Which is what nature does. Our vision is in colour and developed over tens of millions of years to be the finest system available for recording visible light. So give nature a chance. Work with her. Subtle off-whites and off-greys flatter architecture and human beings alike.

62

'Colour is a matter of taste and of sensitivity.'
Edouard Manet

This is the first of two consecutive schemes that use very similar palettes. Both are important examples because they each contain brown of one kind or another and purple of some kind too. These are, it would seem, the two great anchoring colours that dominate not only the palettes in this book but have also come to dominate colour combinations from the early nineteenth century onwards. The bedroom here echoes (albeit faintly) one of the earliest and most famous examples of this combination – a widely publicized scheme for a neo-Greek Napoleonic bedchamber for Parisian society lady, Mme. Recamier.

63

'Colour is all. When colour is right, form is right. Colour is everything, colour is vibration like music; everything is vibration.'
Marc Chagall

Though this is the second of two consecutive palettes that plays with a relationship between blue and brown, the principal lesson to be learned here is from the ceiling.

Throughout this book, you'll have seen many examples of different ways to map colour onto buildings – but, for impact, try painting the ceiling. I once lived in a house with a very high ceiling in a very small dining room, which my landlord painted blood red. The colour appeared to descend about a foot into the room, bringing the ceiling with it. This ceiling, because it is dark, does likewise.

64

'*There are connoisseurs of blue just as there are connoisseurs of wine.*'
Colette

Just as brown can take any colour scheme, tie it down, root it to the floor and – if you're not careful – drag it deep underground, so does brown itself need lifting. It needs to be cheered up from time to time, dressed up and taken out for a spin. Shown a bit of blue sky, perhaps.

The two-colour relationships that keep popping up in this book are red/green and blue/brown. Sometimes that blue is inky or the colour of washed out indigo. Occasionally it is slightly green-tinged and watery. But the blue here is atmospheric. It is a tint of ultramarine which sits slightly to the purple side of the purest blue you can find, cobalt blue. It is one of a happy, elite band of blues that remind you of what the sky can occasionally look like.

65

'Light is therefore colour.'
J.M.W. Turner

The soft, light colours of this temperate palette sensibly demonstrate the fact that, if you take a large section of the colour wheel (here it is a chunk of around 30% from green right round to purple) and then dilute the colours with white to around the same tint, it is surprising just how harmonious the result can be. This is yet another example of the importance of getting the right tonality.

These colours, of course, reflect the bluish wavelengths of Northern light from a cloudy sky or North-facing room. Hence the Scandinavian traditions, from Gustavian decoration through to Carl Larsson, of using tints like these to make rooms appear to glow.

66

'Blue colour is everlastingly appointed by the deity to be a source of delight.'
John Ruskin

Look closely and you'll see that this is one of the most unusual rooms you'll ever have seen. The effect is also beautiful: the walls haven't been painted separately from the floor. Instead the woad tint of blue used for the floor has been sprayed over the skirting board and up the wall in a gently gradated mist that leads to sage green. Clever.

These colours are deeper versions of some of those on the previous page, more Northern light colours which no longer glow here but hum. The green even has the power to change colour. This is because it sits between blue (the tint of Northern daylight) and yellow (the tint of tungsten domestic lighting). Only this blue-green-grey and a number of cool pinks made with red oxide sit on this cusp, giving you the chance to decorate with two – or even three – colours in one. How's that for value?

67

'Who told you that one paints with colours? One makes use of colours, but one paints with emotions.'
Jean-Baptiste-Siméon Chardin

So what's the story here? Is this a red-green thing going on? An orange-green thing? A brown-green vibe instead of the brown-blue usual gig? Well, on the four-colour optical colour wheel on page 151, you'll find that a slightly bluish green aims its complementary sights at orange. So, the sage green and tan that are featured here are a satisfying combination.

If you ask me which are the most satisfying colour schemes of all, I'd have to say the answer is those that place complementary colours together in a subtle way, by toning for example. Every time. And why? Because these are the arrangements which exploit the sensitivity of the receptors in our eyes. And what happens then? Well, that is when our souls dance.

how colour works

HOW COLOUR WORKS

'All students need to know about colour is the basic colour wheel and complementary colours. There are many books on colour theory; do not waste your time and money.'
Sergei Bongart

The following four pages contain various colour models – structures that are used to explain how colours relate to each other and how we perceive them – that are all useful in helping to understand how the palettes in this book work.

Colour models have been in use for millenia; Aristotle developed the first western scale of colours, which in turn influenced Newton's decision to settle on seven colours for the rainbow (he had at various points thought there to be five or eleven). Even modern systems still refer to colour in essentially Newtonian terms.

To an extent all colour models are valid in some way. Even the most sophisticated 3-D colour models in use by scientists still cannot account for some colours, so no one model necessarily reigns supreme; they are all fallible. That's because human vision itself is not consistent and it is not neat. It's not consistent because we each of us are blessed with minutely different configurations of optical receptors in our eyes (the rods and cones). It's not neat because vision is not a logical, but a biological mechanism that has developed as an important tool for a myriad number of human activities: it is analogue, not digital, and its sensitivity to the colours of the rainbow varies (see colour model 3 on page 151).

COLOUR MODEL 1 is the one that we learnt at school. The primary paint colours – which cannot be produced by mixing other colours – are yellow, red and blue and their secondaries are made by intermixing. The result is that when the model is arranged as a circle, the complementary of red is green (being opposite).

Complementaries appear to 'fight' when placed together and when mixed together make brown of some kind. Many of the subtler and more complex colours in the palettes involve the dilution of one colour with a small quantity of its complementary plus the addition of white and/or black. Other palettes pair complementary colours together to deliberate effect. This model is a pragmatic one because it works for pigments and chemical colorants, which in turn are often imperfect. It is also known as the 'subtractive' model because as the colours are mixed, they cancel out a degree of their own luminosity and become darker. So purple and green are less bright than their combined constituent primaries. A case of the sum being less than the parts.

COLOUR MODEL 2 is a four-colour primary model, unusual at first sight but actually formulated as long ago as 1878 by the German physiologist Ewald Hering, who thought that yellow, red, blue and green, together with black and white, formed a palette of six 'natural' colours. This is partly because green is perceived as a colour independent of its component subtractive colours, blue and yellow. (The eye's physiology sets up three signal channels to the brain, each one of opposing colours: black-white, red-green, blue-yellow. Green has its name up there with the others.)

This four-colour palette creates an interesting set of four secondary colours: orange, violet, turquoise and lime green. One result of this, for example, is that the complementary of turquoise becomes orange and you can see a muted example of this complementary relationship in palette 58. The four-colour model was refined in the twentieth century, published and republished and then technically perfected by the Swedish Colour Centre Foundation, who issued it as the Standard Color Atlas of the Natural Color System (NCS), in 1979. It's now adopted as several national standards and by paint and coatings manufacturers worldwide.

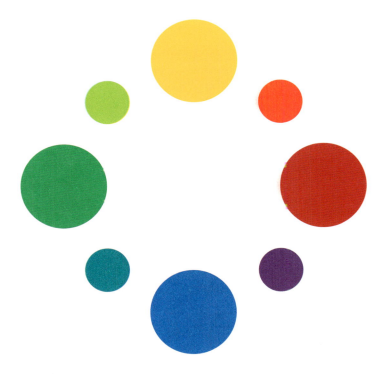

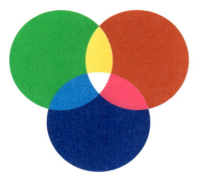

COLOUR MODEL 3 reverts to three primaries and they're different again from colour model 1. The reason is that these are the primary and secondary colours of light: green, warm red and purple-blue light when mixed together produce white light (just as red, yellow and blue paint are supposed to make black but, because of pigment imperfection, make a murky brown). Their secondary colours are also interesting: cyan blue (similar to turquoise), magenta and yellow, which most bizarrely of all is produced by mixing red and green light. Note that because the secondaries result from the addition of two other light colours, they are also more luminous. Not surprisingly, this is called an additive palette.

There is no magic behind the choice of colours and no alchemy in their mixing. The choice of red, green and blue primaries from among the colours of the visible spectrum (i.e. the rainbow) is all down to the way we're built. We perceive a very narrow band of electromagnetic radiation (which includes radio and gamma waves) and we call that visible portion light. The three types of sensor on our retinas that respond to different colours within the visible spectrum have peak sensitivity in different areas: one peaks in the blue part of the spectrum, one in the green and one in the red. If we had sensors that were sensitive to infra-red or ultra-violet (as some animals do) we might see more colours. As it is, because we have only three types (plus one for monochrome vision), our entire colour world is dependent on them: all perceivable colours are made up from various combinations of their activities. That gives us a measly, separately identifiable 16 million colours to play with.

COLOUR MODEL 4 takes the secondary colours of light – cyan, magenta and yellow – and works them backwards. The theory is that if you take three sheets of transparent plastic in these three colours, you should be able to produce the light primaries by subtraction. Thus a sheet of cyan plastic film held over a sheet of magenta plastic film should give a less luminous, but blue light. It works a bit like mixing paint and these theoretical subtractive primaries, cyan, magenta and yellow, ought (in opposition to colour model 3) to make black when overlaid. Of course they don't because coloured plastic, like coloured anything (other than light), is never 100 percent totally purely coloured.

It's the same story with printing inks. This model lies behind modern printing methods, which use cyan, magenta and yellow transparent inks over white paper (a source of reflected light) to reproduce full-colour photographs in books and magazines. In practice, printers also use black to bolster the performance of the three colours and the resulting printing method (which is part-additive, part-subtractive) is known as CMYK process printing, now used worldwide.

But CMYK has always had its weaknesses, notably poor greens and especially oranges, which always look dull and muddy, mainly due, again, to the technical limitations of the inks. Pantone®, one of the largest colour authorities in the world, and certainly the single most persuasive voice in the graphics and printing industries, has solved these problems to a large extent with the introduction of two further ink colours, green and orange, as shown on the left. Together with CMYK they make a six-colour process method called Hexachrome®. This book is one of very few consumer volumes to be printed in Hexachrome®; it was an essential choice for the accurate colour rendering of the palettes and an added advantage in that it reproduces vibrant photographs well.

USEFUL COLOUR TERMS

COMPLEMENTARIES On colour models, complementaries sit on opposite sides of the wheel. In theory they are colours that when mixed in the correct quantities will cancel each other out and produce grey or black (pigments) or white (light). In practice, subtractive, pigment complementaries produce murky browns. Complementary colours when placed against each other will play optical tricks and appear to hover and excite each other (red and green, for example). The three- and four-colour subtractive models (see colour models 1 and 2 on pages 149–150) offer different and interesting arrangements of complementaries; the three-colour additive model (of light primary and secondary colours) offers an arrangement of complementaries with the best optical properties.

HUE The separately identifiable character of a colour, e.g. red, orange-red, orange. The tiny steps around the colour wheel can be measured by the colour's hue and are determined by a colour's wavelength.

CHROMA A reference for the saturation of any hue in relation to an equivalently luminous grey. In other words, the purity or intensity of a colour, not its lightness or darkness or its hue. You can alter the chromatic value of colours on your TV by slowly reducing the picture from full colour to black and white. The Greek word for colour.

TINT Example: a tint of blue is a light blue, blue plus white.

SHADE Example: a shade of blue is a dark blue, blue plus black.

TONE Example: a tone of blue is a greyed blue, blue plus grey.

CUSP COLOUR A relatively new term used to describe those complex (often muddy or greyed colours) which appear to change colour under different lighting conditions. These are therefore colours which do not conform to the cognitive phenomenon of colour memory. Two examples are greyish green-blue and pink made with bluish red oxides. They appear to take on separate chromatic identities when lit with, say, the extremes of warm tungsten lighting and cool bluish light from a densely cloud-covered sky. Because of the tendency of bright daylight to veer between the latter and full spectrum direct sunlight, it is complex colours which inhabit the borders of blue and violet that are likely to be cusp colours.

SATURATION The degree to which colours are intense on the one hand or greyed, tinted or otherwise sullied on the other. A fully saturated colour is one at its most brilliant, pure and intense, a hue. Defined as chroma divided by lightness.

COLOUR MEMORY The phenomenon whereby we ignore visual stimuli and use a memory of a colour to ensure its constancy under varying lighting conditions. A means of ensuring an artificial colour constancy.

THE COLOUR RANGE

This is the complete range of colours that form the basis of all the colour palettes you have just seen. From the left, the colours in this palette are grouped into two-column 'families' of complementary colours, though almost every colour will work with any other in the same row or column. Though this

1 Silica White	16 Verd-Antique	31 Oyster	46 Stone Ochre
2 Platinum Pale	17 Raw Earth	32 Gesso	47 Burnt Verdigris
3 Pearl Ashes	18 Sepia	33 Wax Myrtle	48 Palm Honey
4 Graphite	19 Lime White	34 Tufa	49 Gypsum
5 Plumbago	20 White Ochre	35 Malm	50 Yellow Drab
6 Charcoal	21 Old White	36 Basswood	51 Light Gamboge
7 Bone White	22 Tundra	37 Passion Flower	52 Weld Yellow
8 Alabaster	23 Cobble	38 Ivory	53 Aconite Yellow
9 Oak Apple	24 Antique Earth	39 Travertina Crema	54 Indian Yellow
10 Granite	25 Quartz	40 Ecru	55 Old Cream
11 Antimony	26 Canvas	41 Pumice	56 Pale Coumarin
12 Mercury	27 Parchment	42 Scarab	57 Oxford Ochre
13 Bianco	28 China Clay	43 Marble	58 Sienna Earth
14 Flake White	29 Tuscan Earth	44 White Mulberry	59 Safflower
15 Light Umber	30 Amber Gris	45 Vellum	60 Red Ochre

colour range finds its inspiration in natural, cultural and historic sources, it can (as we have seen in the palettes that precede it) flatter the most modern of spaces. This range, my 'Elements of Colour' collection, is commercially available from Fired Earth. Alternatively, you could take the swatch you wish to match to a paint shop and select from a make of your choice.

61 Chalk White
62 Roman Ochre
63 Coralline
64 Cinnabar Red
65 Cochineal
66 Alizarin Earth
67 Dutch White
68 Old Ochre
69 Pompeiian Red
70 Madder Red
71 Surpar Red
72 Dragon's Blood
73 Pale Saxifrage
74 White Mezereon
75 Orchard Pink

76 Rose Bay
77 Tyrian Rose
78 Carragheen
79 Manna Ash
80 Rose Mallow
81 Chalk Violet
82 Gentian Violet
83 Amethyst
84 Burnt Juniper
85 Pale Cirrus
86 Sea Lavender
87 Welkin Blue
88 Zenith Blue
89 Bamiyan Blue
90 Woad Blue

91 Glass Samphire
92 Blue Ashes
93 Smoke Blue
94 Pale Lapis
95 Mariana Blue
96 Carbon Blue
97 Blue Moon
98 Northern Lights
99 Duck Egg
100 Blue Grass
101 Turkish Blue
102 Andaman Sea
103 Moonstone
104 Opal Green
105 Marram

106 Ultramarine Ashes
107 Weald Green
108 Zangar Green
109 Summer Lichen
110 Celadon
111 Sweet Cicely
112 Absinth
113 Garnet
114 Malachite
115 Pale Verdigris
116 Quince
117 Orchid Leaf
118 Verdilith
119 Oak Fern
120 Wild Olive

PAINT MATCHES

Every colour featured in the colour palette on the previous spread is matched to a paint colour available from my 'Elements of Colour' collection of paints for Fired Earth. Below is a list of every palette in the book with each swatch named and numbered to make matching your chosen colour to a Fired Earth paint easy.

The numbers refer first to the palette and then to the individual colours within that palette. So, for example, the zingy mustard that is the second numbered swatch in palette 58 (page 127) can – with a quick glance at the list below – be easily identified as Indian Yellow. To enable you to match the colours with the minimum of fuss, the number in brackets refers to the number attributed to each colour within the Fired Earth 'Elements of Colour' collection.

Palette 1 1 Bone White (17) 2 China Clay (28) 3 Madder Red (70) 4 Garnet (113)

Palette 2 1 Cinnabar Red (64) 2 Pale Cirrus (85) 3 Pale Lapis (94) 4 Absinth (112) 5 Garnet (113) 6 Verdilith (118)

Palette 3 1 Safflower (59) 2 Turkish Blue (101) 3 Zangar Green (108) 4 Garnet (113) 5 Verdilith (118) 6 Oak Fern (119)

Palette 4 1 Alizarin Earth (66) 2 Burnt Juniper (84) 3 Celadon (110) 4 Sweet Cicely (111)

Palette 5 1 Duck Egg (99) 2 Blue Grass (100) 3 Andaman Sea (102) 4 Weald Green (107) 5 Zangar Green (108) 6 Garnet (113) 7 Malachite (114)

Palette 6 1 Pearl Ashes (3) 2 Charcoal (6) 3 Pale Cirrus (85) 4 Oak Fern (119)

Palette 7 1 Oak Apple (9) 2 Granite (10) 3 Antimony (11) 4 Pale Cirrus (85) 5 Garnet (113) 6 Orchid Leaf (117)

Palette 8 1 Verd-Antique (16) 2 Raw Earth (17) 3 Antique Earth (24) 4 Garnet (113) 5 Sweet Cicely (111)

Palette 9 1 Antique Earth (24) 2 Weald Green (107) 3 Pale Verdigris (115) 4 Orchid Leaf (117) 5 Oak Fern (119) 6 Chalk Violet (81)

Palette 10 1 Pearl Ashes (3) 2 Alabaster (8) 3 Granite (10) 4 Antimony (11)

Palette 11 1 Oak Apple (9) 2 Granite (10) 3 Antimony (11) 4 Tuscan Earth (29) 5 Safflower (59) 6 Red Ochre (60)

Palette 12 1 Marram (105) 2 Zangar Green (108) 3 Celadon (110) 4 Absinth (112) 5 Garnet (113)

Palette 13 1 Coralline (63) 2 Old Ochre (68) 3 White Mezereon (74) 4 Turkish Blue (101)

Palette 14 1 Mercury (12) 2 Basswood (36) 3 Burnt Juniper (84) 4 Blue Ashes (92)

Palette 15 1 Stone Ochre (46) 2 Burnt Verdigris (47) 3 Amethyst (83) 4 Burnt Juniper (84) 5 Bamiyan Blue (89)

Palette 16 1 Plumbago (5) 2 Antimony (11) 3 Mercury (12) 4 Tuscan Earth (29)

Palette 17 1 Antique Earth (24) 2 Amber Gris (30) 3 Scarab (42) 4 Sea Lavender (86) 5 Zenith Blue (88) 6 Bamiyan Blue (89)

Palette 18 1 Oak Apple (9) 2 Basswood (36) 3 Welkin Blue (87) 4 Bamiyan Blue (89) 5 Carbon Blue (96) 6 Andaman Sea (102)

Palette 19 1 Amber Gris (30) 2 Burnt Juniper (84) 3 Bamiyan Blue (89) 4 Blue Ashes (92) 5 Smoke Blue (93)

Palette 20 1 Charcoal (6) 2 Gentian Violet (82) 3 Amethyst (83) 4 Sea Lavender (86) 5 Turkish Blue (101) 6 Andaman Sea (102)

Palette 21 1 Platinum Pale (2) 2 Manna Ash (79) 3 Chalk Violet (81) 4 Mariana Blue (95) 5 Zenith Blue (88) 6 Bamiyan Blue (89)

Palette 22 1 Pearl Ashes (3) 2 Pompeiian Red (69) 3 Tyrian Rose (77) 4 Burnt Juniper (84) 5 Carbon Blue (96)

Palette 23 1 Red Ochre (60) 2 Chalk Violet (81) 3 Gentian Violet (82) 4 Burnt Juniper (84) 5 Carragheen (78) 6 Amethyst (83)

Palette 24 1 Alabaster (8) 2 Raw Earth (17) 3 Zenith Blue (88) 4 Quince (116) 5 Orchard Pink (75) 6 Chalk Violet (81)

Palette 25 1 Charcoal (6) 2 Weld Yellow (52) 3 Rose Mallow (80) 4 White Mezereon (74) 5 Rose Bay (76)

Palette 26 1 Charcoal (6) 2 Antimony (11) 3 Light Umber (15) 4 Rose Bay (76) 5 Parchment (27)

Palette 27 1 Granite (10) 2 Antimony (11) 3 Raw Earth (17)

Palette 28 1 Sepia (18) 2 Orchard Pink (75) 3 Rose Bay (76) 4 Sea Lavender (86) 5 Zenith Blue (88)

Palette 29 1 Light Gamboge (51) 2 Chalk Violet (81) 3 Ultramarine Ashes (106) 4 Granite (10) 5 Orchid Leaf (117)

Palette 30 1 Granite (10) 2 Ecru (40) 3 Amethyst (83) 4 Bamiyan Blue (89)

Palette 31 1 Aconite Yellow (53) 2 Indian Yellow (54) 3 Safflower (59) 4 Alizarin Earth (66)

Palette 32 1 Sienna Earth (58) 2 Safflower (59) 3 Cochineal (65) 4 Madder Red (70) 5 Surpar Red (71) 6 Gentian Violet (82) 7 Bamiyan Blue (89) 8 Andaman Sea (102)

Palette 33 1 Plumbago (5) 2 Sienna Earth (58) 3 Safflower (59) 4 Cinnabar Red (64) 5 Tyrian Rose (77) 6 Bamiyan Blue (89)

Palette 34 1 Antimony (11) 2 Sepia (18) 3 Alizarin Earth (66) 4 Madder Red (70) 5 Blue Ashes (92)

Palette 35 1 Basswood (36) 2 Yellow Drab (50) 3 Cochineal (65) 4 Manna Ash (79) 5 Welkin Blue (87) 6 Blue Ashes (92)

Palette 36 1 Alizarin Earth (66) 2 Welkin Blue (87) 3 Zenith Blue (88) 4 Moonstone (103)

Palette 37 1 Bone White (7) 2 Raw Earth (17) 3 Tuscan Earth (29) 4 Malm (35) 5 White Ochre (20) 6 Red Ochre (60)

Palette 38 1 Charcoal (6) 2 Sepia (18) 3 Light Gamboge (51) 4 Weld Yellow (52) 5 Cinnabar Red (64)

Palette 39 1 Cinnabar Red (64) 2 Madder Red (70) 3 Surpar Red (71) 4 Dragon's Blood (72)

Palette 40 1 Bone White (7) 2 Oak Apple (9) 3 Granite (10) 4 Malm (35) 5 Alizarin Earth (66) 6 Orchard Pink (75)

Palette 41 1 Amber Gris (30) 2 Burnt Verdigris (47) 3 Weld Yellow (52) 4 Safflower (59) 5 Aconite Yellow (53) 6 Rose Mallow (80) 7 Welkin Blue (87)

Palette 42 1 Mercury (12) 2 Indian Yellow (54) 3 Sienna Earth (58) 4 Coralline (63) 5 Alizarin Earth (66) 6 Turkish Blue (101)

Palette 43 1 Antimony (11) 2 Gypsum (49) 3 Yellow Drab (50) 4 Welkin Blue (87) 5 Smoke Blue (93) 6 Pale Lapis (94)

Palette 44 1 Cobble (23) 2 Antique Earth (24) 3 Travertina Crema (39) 4 Gypsum (49) 5 Chalk White (61) 6 Sea Lavender (86) 7 Welkin Blue (87) 8 Glass Samphire (91)

Palette 45 1 Granite (10) 2 Canvas (26)
3 Yellow Drab (50) 4 Pompeiian Red
(69) 5 Surpar Red (71) 6 Smoke Blue
(93)

Palette 46 1 Wax Myrtle (33) 2 Pumice
(41) 3 Palm Honey (48) 4 Sienna Earth
(58)

Palette 47 1 Sepia (18) 2 Tuscan Earth
(29) 3 Stone Ochre (46) 4 Indian Yellow
(54) 5 Bamiyan Blue (89)

Palette 48 1 Oak Apple (9) 2 Wax Myrtle
(33) 3 Basswood (36) 4 Ecru (40) 5
Coralline (63) 6 Zenith Blue (88)

Palette 49 1 Flake White (14) 2 Canvas
(26) 3 Basswood (36) 4 Aconite Yellow
(53) 5 Safflower (59) 6 Red Ochre (60)
7 Pompeiian Red (69) 8 Orchard Pink
(75)

Palette 50 1 Light Umber (15) 2
Basswood (36) 3 Old Ochre (68) 4
Orchard Pink (75) 5 Chalk Violet (81) 6
Zenith Blue (88)

Palette 51 1 Pearl Ashes (3) 2 Granite
(10) 3 Sepia (18) 4 Tundra (22) 5
Amber Gris (30) 6 Scarab (42) 7 Palm
Honey (48)

Palette 52 1 Sea Lavender (86) 2 Zenith
Blue (88) 3 Blue Ashes (92) 4 Marram
(105) 5 Pale Verdigris (115) 6 Gypsum
(49)

Palette 53 1 Pumice (41) 2 Stone Ochre
(46) 3 Cinnabar Red (64) 4 Ultramarine
Ashes (106) 5 Zangar Green (108) 6
Quince (116)

Palette 54 1 Tyrian Rose (77) 2 Gentian
Violet (82) 3 Bamiyan Blue (89) 4
Turkish Blue (101)

Palette 55 1 Pearl Ashes (3) 2 Oak Apple
(9) 3 Malm (35) 4 Cinnabar Red (64)
5 Safflower (59) 6 Bamiyan Blue (89)

Palette 56 1 Safflower (59) 2 Red Ochre
(60) 3 Mariana Blue (95) 4 Turkish
Blue (101)

Palette 57 1 Graphite (4) 2 Raw Earth
(17) 3 Aconite Yellow (53) 4 Orchard
Pink (75) 5 Duck Egg (99) 6 Moonstone
(103)

Palette 58 1 Palm Honey (48) 2 Indian
Yellow (54) 3 Pale Lapis (94)

Palette 59 1 Antimony (11) 2 Mercury
(12) 3 Madder Red (70) 4 Tyrian Rose
(77) 5 Sweet Cicely (111)

Palette 60 1 White Mulberry (44) 2
Antimony (11) 3 Pale Cirrus (85) 4
Glass Samphire (91)

Palette 61 1 Platinum Pale (2) 2 Pearl
Ashes (3) 3 Plumbago (5) 4 Antimony
(11) 5 Pale Cirrus (85)

Palette 62 1 Raw Earth (17) 2 Basswood
(36) 3 Gentian Violet (82) 4 Amethyst
(83) 5 Sea Lavender (86) 6 Zenith Blue
(88) 7 Woad Blue (90)

Palette 63 1 Antimony (11) 2 Raw Earth
(17) 3 Gentian Violet (82) 4 Burnt
Juniper (84) 5 Zenith Blue (88) 6 Woad
Blue (90) 7 Blue Ashes (92)

Palette 64 1 Carragheen (78) 2 Manna
Ash (79) 3 Burnt Juniper (84) 4 Welkin
Blue (87)

Palette 65 1 Pale Cirrus (85) 2 Sea
Lavender (86) 3 Glass Samphire (91) 4
Blue Moon (97) 5 Northern Lights (98)
6 Moonstone (103) 7 Opal Green (104)

Palette 66 1 Vellum (45) 2 Light
Gamboge (51) 3 Zenith Blue (88) 4
Bamiyan Blue (89) 5 Blue Grass (100)
6 Ultramarine Ashes (106)

Palette 67 1 Safflower (59) 2 Red Ochre
(60) 3 Weald Green (107) 4 Sweet
Cicely (111)

PICTURE CREDITS

2-3 Narratives/Jan Baldwin; 4-5 Narratives/Jan Baldwin/Alastair Hendy; 10-11 Narratives/Emma Lee; 13 Mainstreamimages/Paul Massey; 14-15 The Interior Archive/Simon Upton designer Ilaria Miani; 16-17 Simon Kenny/CONTENT/Jake Dowse Architects, stylist; Georgi Waddy; 18 Camera Press/Côté Sud/Nicolas Tosi; 21 Minh + Wass; 23 Richard Powers; 25 Taverne Agency/John Drummer, Stylist: Karin Draajer; 26 Camera Press/Côté Sud/Nicolas Tosi; 28 Narratives Jan Baldwin; 30 Camera Press/Côté Sud/Bernard Touillon; 33 Richard Powers/Marmol Radziner Architects; 34 Taverne Agency/ Karina Tengberg, Stylist: Tami Christiansen; 36-37 Narratives/Jan Baldwin; 39 Narratives/Jan Baldwin/Alastair Hendy; 40 Julian Wass; 42-43 View/Hufton & Crow; 44 Taverne Agency/Nathalie Krag, Stylist: Letizia Donati; 46 The Interior Archive Simon Upton designer Ilaria Miani; 48 Tavene Agency/Anna de Leeuw, Stylist: Marianne Luning; 51 The Interior Archive/Simon Upton designer designer Miles Redd; 53 Taverne Agency/Anna de Leuw/Stylist, Marianne Luning: 55 Camera Press/Maison Francaise/J M Palisse; 56 Richard Powers designer Mary Wilson; 59 Taverne Agency/Alexander van Berge, stylist: Marianne van Heusden; 60 Taverne Agency Ngoc Minh Ngo; 63 Taverne Agency/Lisa Cohen, Stylist:Fiona Mcarthy; 65 Taverne Agency/Alexander van Berge, Stylist: Marianne van Heusden; 66-67 The Interior Archive/Edina van der Wyck; 68-69 Narratives/Jan Baldwin; 70 Camera Press/Maison /Française/Christophe Dugied; 72 The Interior Archive/Luke White architect David Mikhail; 75 The Interior Archive/Simon Upton/designer Ilaria Miani; 77 Photozest Inside/D. Ross/H&L; 78 Geoff Lung/f8 photo library; 81 Narratives/Emma Lee/designer Emma Bridgewater; 82 Camera Press/Côté Sud/Nicolas Tosi; 84-85 Deidi von Schaewen designer Laurie Owen, Johannesburg; 86-87 Narratives/A Mezza & E Escalante/ Architect Martin Facundo Cinquegrani; 88-89 David Gilles designer Ann Louise Roswald; 91 Camera Press/Côté Ouest/Christophe Dugied; 92-93 Photozest /Inside/designer Helen Portugal; 95 Photozest/Inside/Architect Mark Mack; 96-97 Narratives/Emma Lee; 99 Narratives/Emma Lee; 100-101 The Interior Archive/Simon Upton/:designer Ilaria Miani 102-103 Photozest/Inside/W Waldron/ Architect Welliver; 105 Minh + Wass/Drake Design Associates; 107 Narrataives/Paul Raeside; 109 Camera Press/ Côté Sud/Henri del Olmo; 110 Richard Powers/Kim Utzon Architect; 113 Deidi von Schaewen, the Lofthotel, Murg Walensee, Switzerland; 115 Taverne Agency/Earl Carter/stylist Anne Marie Kiely; 117 Richard Powers designers Lawson & Fenning; 118 Ngoc Minh Ngo designer Sherry Olsen; 120 The Interior Archive/Nicolas Matheus architect Philippe Phi, stylist Laurence Dougier; 123 Redcover.com/Chris Tubbs; 124 Taverne Agency/Earl Carter/Stylist Anne-Marie Kiely;126 Redcover.com/James Mitchell; 128 Andreas von Einsiedel/ designer David Carter; 130 Camera Press /MCM/J Oppenheim/D Rozensztroch; 132 Côté Sud/Bernard Touillon; 135 Camera Press/Maison Francaise/J M Palisse; 136 Camera Press/Catherine Panchouf; 139 Richard Powers/designer Sue Hosteler; 141 Narratives/Jan Baldwin/Lena Proudlock; 142 Narratives/Polly Eltes/designer Abigail Ahern; 144 Richard Powers/designer Kay Kollar; 147-148 Simon Kenny/ CONTENT/Jake Dowse Architects,stylist: Georgi Waddy.

COLOUR ACCURACY AND THE LIMITATIONS OF THIS BOOK

This volume has been printed in Hexachrome®, an advanced printing process that uses six component colours rather than the conventional four. While Hexachrome® offers over 3,000 controllable colours, there are still some limitations and variations within the printing process. As a result, it is impossible to guarantee the fidelity of the colours reproduced.

The printed swatches in this book have been matched to Fired Earth's Kevin MᶜCloud Elements of Colour paint collection using the paint manufacturers' colour card. However, neither the author nor the publisher can take responsibility for any discrepancies in colour between a swatch colour in this book and a specified Fired Earth colour.

It is important to note that different batches of paint from any manufacturer will vary minutely in colour. When buying paint, always check the batch numbers on the tin and buy from the same batch whenever possible. If it is not possible to buy from the same batch, mix the tins to achieve a uniform colour.

For more advice on paint matching and to buy the best of British branded paint, visit www.choosingpaint.com

First published in 2009 by
Quadrille Publishing Ltd
Alhambra House
27–31 Charing Cross Road
London WC2H 0LS
www.quadrille.co.uk

Editorial Director Anne Furniss

Creative Director Helen Lewis

Editor Simon Davis

Designer Nicola Davidson

Picture Research Nadine Bazar
Sarah Airey

Picture Co-ordinator Samantha Rolfe

Production Director Vincent Smith

Production Controller Ruth Deary

Text and palettes © Kevin MᶜCloud 2009

Design and layout © Quadrille Publishing Ltd 2009

The rights of Kevin MᶜCloud to be identified as the author of this work have been asserted by him in accordance with the Copyright, Design and Patents Act 1988.

Cataloguing-in-Publication Data: a catalogue record for this book is available from the British Library.

ISBN 978 1 84400 699 1

Printed and bound in China